MW01242965

HOLDING SPACE TO HEAL

A Conversation with Holly Ramey

Heather Sanderson

Majestic Wisdom Publishing

CONTENTS

PREFACE

When I started the Majestic Wisdom podcast in October 2020, I had no intention of turning the episodes into short books. I wanted to share conversations that I had with friends, teachers, and people I met who influenced and inspired me, so that others could also hear them. Having never listened to a podcast, and with very little sound editing experience, I set out to learn along the way. What I learned most is how much I love listening to people as they drop into the vulnerability of their heart, sharing openly and authentically from that place. It's truly beautiful.

We each have wisdom to share, and, from the outset, the goal of the podcast was to speak with people who, through their vision, dreams, passion, work, and creativity, embody wise ways of being for modern living. The process is very organic. People I know well, or have just met, will spark a feeling of resonance and light in my heart, and I'll ask if they're interested in co-creating an episode. Rarely, people I've never met reach out, their presence and magic nudging us into a collaboration. This book you have in your hands started the same way the podcast started—by following a thread of an idea.

About eight months after launching the podcast, I

felt the energy of an idea floating around me: to turn the first podcast episode with Stewart Hoyt into a book. Unsure, I listed out all the complicating factors as to why this shouldn't be: getting permission from the collaborators, figuring out royalties, and the big one—how could I make the conversation work as a book? I placed enough hurdles in the way to talk myself out of trying. The idea popped up every so often and I brushed it aside until, in February 2022, the thought of making a book resurfaced again. This time with more intensity. This time I acquiesced and said yes, realizing that there are so many great thoughts and perspectives communicated in the podcasts, and they wanted to be shared with more people in another form!

So, here we are! (Now on book three of the series which I've called "The Future is Possible"). The process of creating that first book from a conversation was a brand-new, creative experience for me, and one that has been surprisingly engaging, exciting, and even overstimulating! Once the audio was transcribed into Word, it was fascinating to see patterns of speech on the page. The "if, if, ifs," and "you knows," and half formed sentences, trailing off into...

While leaving the words and integrity of the speaker's voice intact, I focused with great care on editing the conversation. Removing idioms, expressions, repetitions, and the attempts at formulating an idea three or four times before it emerges, fully formed, reminded me of removing the husk from a cob of corn. As the layers and patterns of speech were peeled back and away, a beautiful, nourishing, whole kernel of wisdom and truth was revealed. This process cracked open new ways of thinking about language; how different writing is to speaking, and the different expectations of a listener to those of a reader. Listeners, in general, are more able to accept those quirks of speaking that each of us has, whereas readers tend to need more compliance to the rules of grammar and concision that are hard to accomplish in a conversation. This further emphasized the question: how will this work as a book? Only now, instead of dismissing the idea or quitting, it became a mission—one that has been highly generative and productive in the best possible ways.

Engaged by the problem-solving quest, answers kept coming on how to make this work. Once the conversation was cleaned up, so many options emerged in the form of structure. This was basic at first, like adding chapter headings, a question or two to break up longer soliloquies, and then expanded to creating additional pieces that don't exist in the podcast: this preface, the introduction, key concepts, footnotes, ways to inspire readers to engage with the conversation in the form of worksheets and synthesizing it all together in conclusion. Turns out, I committed to taking one thing and helping it transform into something new. I am grateful to be the midwife of this rebirth, and I hope that within these pages you also find something transformative.

INTRODUCTION

"Holding space" is a term that is used and heard a lot in healing and teaching communities. Like the jargon or acronyms of any community or organization spoken ubiquitously (and which make sense to those who know the language used within a group), the term "holding space," often creates confusion to those who have never encountered the concept. Shared vocabulary and language are an important part of belonging and feeling safe. As you read this book, it's helpful to understand what is meant by "holding space" because it's important for you to hold it, too, as you explore your responses to the conversation and concepts you are about to encounter.

Holly Ramey and I met at breakfast in Mumbai (Bombay), India in 2014. It was the first day of a retreat with our yoga teacher, Mona Anand, and I didn't know a single person on the trip aside from Mona. Nervous to join in with the others, I was relieved by Holly's welcoming face and warm "good morning" as, with an inviting sweep of her arm, she asked me to sit with her. Once seated, my breath and body relaxed and, in the matter of a few moments, we dropped into a deep conversation about different parts of our healing journeys. The plants (nettle and oatstraw) also came into the conversation as she and I simultaneously deciphered and tried delicious Indian breakfast foods and gorged on masala chai. Even then, perhaps without thinking about it, Holly and I knew how to hold space for one another. We have been doing it ever since, and for that I am truly grateful. The core essence of holding space is to create an environment or encounter where everyone involved feels safe as themselves, whatever their emotional, energetic, and psychological states are in that moment.

Simply put, to hold space is to be present with yourself and/or others without judgment while understanding that everyone works with challenges, difficulty, psychology, processing the world, or trauma. As a yoga teacher, I hold the space for students so that they can feel safe enough to inhabit their bodies, to move and express themselves on the mat. In doing so, I can't know what has happened in every student's life or meet the needs required to ensure everyone's safety in the world outside of class. Nor can I control the larger collective backdrop of their experiences of violence, racism, genderism, sexism, ageism, ableism, classism, and all other forms of subtle or outright attack. I can, when people come to a class, offer my full attention and ability to witness and listen—not just to their words but to their energy and movements—without trying to problem solve, offer an opinion, or fix their experience. I can strive, through my verbal and energetic communication, to generate a safe place for others to be seen, heard, move, or be still for the hour or two that we are together. To be seen and/or heard just as you are, in safety, is incredibly transformative and healing.

Holding space, then, is an active way of witnessing and listening on every level while also removing your ego from the interaction. Safety is created when you know the person you are sharing something with won't repeat it or gossip about it to anyone else. It's also up to the person for whom the space is held to initiate a conversation about what has occurred and what has been shared if they choose to in the future. This means they are in control and won't be caught off guard by someone bringing up something unexpectedly or replanting an experience which may already have been processed and released. If you are holding space for someone else, there is no need to rehash or check in at a later time (unless they invite you to do so). Think of holding space as having an embedded confidentiality clause within it and honor that for yourself and others.

Why is this important? When someone feels safe, they are more able to be in the present moment. From this place of presence, they can then make choices informed by their current experience: to give voice to a conversation and know it's okay to remain silent, to access the deep rest they are lacking from being on guard or from continuous effort. In this space they can feel any emotions which may wish to be expressed (and released), notice patterns of thought, explore different parts of themselves, gain new insights, and/or take reasonable risks to try something new. Safety and support afford the opportunity to excavate past moments of trauma or held emotions and energetic patterns so that they no longer take up space inside of you or run parts of your life. To be held in safe space also means you don't have to do or change anything at all and to trust that you are accepted exactly as you are by others (and yourself) unless there is some part of you that wants to shift.

Having space held for you (and learning to hold it for yourself) can lead to discovering the built up energy that has been stored in the body as grief, sadness, anger, fear, panic, depression, harmful or violent behavior and beliefs and thoughts, to name a few possibilities. It also affords the opportunity to enter and, at the same time, not only focus on wounded aspects of yourself, but on the amazing, beaming, bright qualities and energies which are also crucial parts of your being and are all too often neglected or paved over. Being held allows you to find your way back to your true, authentic Self and all that encompasses, even as it shifts again and again. Holding space helps you to shed whatever energy that has clouded your essential Self.

Imagine now that you don't have anywhere to be held, or can't do it for yourself. Perhaps being in your body doesn't feel solid or safe, or you seek this kind of space but find it's filled with people who talk about you when you aren't there, or aren't paying any attention to you. How does that make you feel? What actions might you take as a result? Perhaps you start to conform or contort yourself to the edges of the space, trying to be invisible, or maybe you become excessively confrontational to make sense of the lack of safety—to put it in its place so you can dominate it. Holding and experiencing held space goes beyond conversations and movement and into the multi-layered depth of our psyche and psychology; on the individual, micro level and collective, macro level, it is about our overall ability to be safe here on the planet and how we behave, consciously or not, when this space is available (or missing).

In the conversation you are about to read, Holly guides us through how she discovered the Tarot and where it has taken her, her work in other healing practices, and a pivotal move from New York City to Nashville, Tennessee during the same time she became a new mother. Holly shows us with skill how she has been held and how she has learned ways to hold space for herself, and discusses her deep longing and commitment to create and hold space for others.

Holly is also unafraid to talk about the dark night of the soul, what that means, how she understands working with both darkness and light, and that holding space is multidimensional: it often includes working with space, time, psychic abilities, energy, spirit, and guides—traveling through and existing in many worlds at once. She reminds me that in healing arts we tend to focus so much on the wounded aspects of Self, or those parts that are out of balance or "off," that it is easy to forget to focus on what is working, and how there is always light, even when it feels impossible to allow or believe.

Part of our conversation includes a plant spirit reading, offered by me. In this case, it's a plant whose energy and spirit can help Holly (and others) with the deep work of holding the light even in the darkness. The plants come to me intuitively, thanks to years of training in Sacred Plant Medicine with Carole Guyett, and by being open to connecting with them. I often feel their energy around me or see an image of the plant in my mind's eye when they want to share some information. Including the plants in the conversation helps get out of the human-centric mindset that so many of us often find ourselves in, helps rebalance the relationship between plants and humans, and adds another layer of inquiry and support. This may be a new concept for some, and I invite and encourage you to stay open to the possibility that humans and plants can co-create together on many levels and be open to the possibility that plants hold space for humans all the time, and they ask us to do the same for them.

As you read, you are invited to make notes for your own self-reflection and purpose, take breaks, and find ways to support yourself. Notice any emotions that surface within you and, if you feel safe to do so, put the book down and sit with or feel those emotions. You don't need to identify what they are, just see what energy is moving within the structure that is you. See what happens when you shed some of your own light upon that which is present. And, as always, take the parts of this book that resonate for you and leave the rest.

KEY CONCEPTS

Some of the concepts in the conversation that follows may be new to you, can't be found in the dictionary, or are meant differently than the definitions you'll find there or in a Google search. Words, language, and definitions evolve as humans explore and experiment, which is an essential part of shifting how we live, create, and envision ourselves and the world around us. With this context in mind, here are a few terms that may be of interest to contemplate further while you read. You may have additional interpretations to add to these concepts, too.

Archetype

An archetype is an energy that is known both individually and collectively; an energy that is large enough and repetitive enough to become something that has a universal understanding that people then try to make sense of in a myriad of ways including myth, the creation of gods and goddesses who embody (or are) one of these energies, and as a way to understand one another.

Archetypal energy can also be seen, from a healing perspective as a part of the personal and collective unconscious that guides our actions/thoughts/ feelings (often subconsciously or unconsciously). It's neutral energy in its purest form, and it takes on a power when it becomes repressed. It can come to control or dominate us without us being aware. The same is true for beliefs we hold about ourselves in the unconscious. If an archetypal energy appears that we are uncomfortable with, we submerge it into the "shadow" of ourselves. This can happen to the point where we almost (or do) lose awareness of it, but it never disappears. The energetic traits lodged in the sub or unconscious then begin to rule us.

For example, if you hold onto the archetypal belief that you're "the damsel in distress" or "the victim," you will always search for clues that support that belief and may even throw yourself into situations that allow you to become "the damsel in distress" (and think you need to be rescued by a "hero" only to be shattered when one doesn't arrive, thus reinforcing the archetype). These archetypes play out through us and around us all the time and, through conscious awareness, or embracing these energies within us, they can become healthy allies for functioning in the world. The "damsel in distress," (through love, acknowledgment, and trying new approaches to situations) can transform into an empowered energy who understands when to seek balanced support from others and when to save yourself; thus no longer playing into the victim dynamic of the "ever-suffering one," "the powerless one," or maintaining a belief that feminine energy is subservient.

You may even transform the "damsel in distress" energy into another overpowering archetype of "the saint," "the martyr," "the tyrant," or "the protector" as part of processing and exploring the layers of archetypal energies that work their way through you on your path of self-discovery. None of these energies are "good" or "bad," they simply show you parts of your consciousness.

The key is to work *with* the energy that serves you instead of letting the archetype itself blindly run you; to have power of autonomy in this relationship with it instead of allowing the archetype to overpower you. There are countless examples of archetypes; everyone embodies several of them, and some more dominant than others. It's up to each person to learn what feels aligned and healthy or unhealthy, in relation to the archetypes that move through them, and to understand that the transformation is never done, but always evolving. You will find several archetypes in the Major Arcana of the Tarot (described later in this section).

Ceremony

Ceremony is an active way for an individual and/ or community to connect with and co-create with spirit and/or other people with a specific intention. A wedding ceremony or funeral function as ways for people to engage with others and interact around a sacred event. Ceremony also exists beyond these somewhat typified expectations of what it means. In the conversation, you will hear more about this as Holly shares her experience of creating and offering new and full moon ceremonies, both virtually and in person.

Ceremony can occur around a personal or communal cycle, such as lunar points in time. Fire festivals around the solstices, equinoxes, and cross-quarter holidays (meaning the moment halfway between each solstice and equinox) have been marked with ceremonies for centuries across Ireland and other lands, each time having its own specific purpose. There are also countless initiation rites of passage and ceremonies performed either within a community or individually, across every culture on the planet and new ones are being created all the time. From a healing perspective, ceremony functions as a way to blend both the physical and spiritual or "other" world and allows a safe space for the person or people engaging in the ceremony to merge with spirit in some way, gain information, and bring it back into everyday awareness so that it can be incorporated it into daily life.

Channel/Channeling

To channel means to receive information (which is otherwise invisible) into your awareness, body, and/or being. This could include energy, vibrations, frequencies, or messages from spirits: nature/ elemental, human, or other. This often happens in a ceremony, and can also occur at any time. Once received, the person who has channeled the information interprets it in different ways, depending on their clair senses (or ways of reading and receiving otherwise "invisible" energy and vibrations). Energy healing modalities such as Reiki are also channeled—the Reiki practitioner is taught to receive Reiki energy and bring it down into the body and energy field of themselves and/or another to help facilitate a balanced flow of energy. The clair senses and Reiki are other key concepts we'll explore in this section.

The Clair Senses

The clair senses are generally known as: clairaudience, clairalience, claircognizance, clairsentience, and clairvoyance. I'm going to add one more: clairvocal. These terms each have their own function (outlined below) and you can think of them collectively as the ability to receive information through sensation, vibration, or intuitive knowing. This information or "raw data" taken into a person's body and awareness from the external world (be it an interaction with another person, animal, a group, plants, land, energy, or spirit) is then interpreted internally in different ways, through the energetic field or psychic ability and awareness a person possesses. These ways of receiving information can occur when you are in an altered state of consciousness or a trance-state induced by meditation, dance, chanting, focusing on something to withdraw all other senses, or what some call "dropping in" to another way of perceiving the world, often done in ceremony, and/or can occur as part of everyday life and normal waking awareness.

Many dictionaries, encyclopedias, and popular thoughts consider these sensory experiences to be paranormal, extraordinary, or supernatural. However, these way of accessing knowledge beyond the physical senses (sight, sound, taste, smell, touch) are entirely normal, ordinary, and natural aspects of every human. They have been, in Western cultures and non-indigenous mindsets, at least, conditioned out of us over centuries of misunderstanding, intolerance, and persecution, which persists today even in the accusatory way in which the dictionary definitions are written. For example, the *Cambridge Dictionary* defines clairvoyance as "claiming to have powers to see the future or see things that other people cannot see." Talk about a definition that does not hold safe space. Right away the word "claiming" suggests that it isn't possible, or it is untrue and goes on to view this completely natural way of perceiving information as a "power" (therefore supernatural) and then untrustworthy because others cannot see it (so it must not be possible or true).

Imagine, if you are someone who possesses one, some, or all these ways of taking in and making sense of the world—how safe would you feel to have them immediately discounted not only by popular culture and dominant beliefs, but also by people you know? Paranormal and supernatural are terms defined as "not scientifically explainable"[1] or "beyond the scope of scientific understanding."[2] These definitions are neutral and true. Yet, there is a long-held bias which equates the belief that if something cannot be proven or duplicated on demand, then it doesn't exist or isn't possible. This is untrue, exclusionary, and extremely harmful. There are many ways of sensing and understanding both the physical/seen and psychic/unseen or "invisible" worlds. Here are brief introductions to the common terms for the clair senses, and you'll hear more about how they relate to working with the Tarot or other healing arts in our conversation. As you read, see if there are any you may encounter or possess:

Clairaudience: the ability for a person to hear frequencies, tones, sounds, or voices beyond what is physically present in their everyday awareness. For example, you may hear (and I have!) the atonal voices of standing stones or your cat's meow when you are miles away from home. This can also apply to hearing energy or spirits (be they elemental or nature beings, guides, ancestors, or spirits moving through a space you're in).

Clairalience: the ability for a person to acquire knowledge by smelling a scent that arises without the source of that scent being physically present. For example, you may smell lavender in a room where there isn't any as a clue for when you need to pay attention to your spiritual wellness, or when encountering a particular energy, spirit, or message from beyond the physical world.

Clairgustance: the ability to taste a substance without putting it in your mouth or to have a taste appear in your mouth when encountering a particular energy or spirit.

Clairecognizance: the ability for a person to acquire psychic knowledge without knowing how or why they know it. The information arrives, perhaps as a feeling, or an intuitive knowing and it can be an insight, about another person, place, or yourself. For example, I've known many times the exact moment a friend on the other side of the planet is giving birth, has lost their job, etc. Who knows how? It simply comes to me: they enter my conscious awareness, and I later confirm it to be true.

Clairsentience: the ability to sense or feel information in your body. For example, you might sense in your body what is happening in the body of another person. If you are with someone having heart surgery, you might feel your heart ache as theirs heals. You become a circuit of energy, attuned to what is happening in the body of another.

Sometimes the translation is exact: a feeling in a particular body part which correlates to theirs, and other times it's a general feeling: nausea, dizziness, or sharpness. Anything really. This happens in sessions with Reiki and massage clients as well and is true for many healing arts practitioners, though you don't have to be trained in any way to receive this kind of sensory information in your own body.

You can also notice sensations in your body when encountering an energy or spirit; perhaps it feels hot or cold, you have tingling sensations around you, or you feel a solidity in the seemingly empty air.

Clairvocal: the ability to receive and interpret energy of the land, nature spirits, and other kinds of spirit, frequency, vibration, and/or energy around you orally by emitting sound. This is also called toning.

Clairvoyance: many believe this has to do with the psychic ability to see the future and, while that is entirely possible, clairvoyance is much broader than that definition as it has to do with the ability to see beyond what is physically present or apparent. Some people may see energy around the body as a color, some may receive images, words, or memories when in the presence of another being, land or space, or on their own. This is often considered to be imagination, but there is a difference. With your imagination you might create something that isn't real, whereas clairvoyance is the ability to interpret actual vibrations, energy, or spiritual information, which is otherwise invisible or unseen, visually. Sometimes this is seen with your eyes, sometimes with your third eye (or a combination of the two).

When I see this kind of information in daily life, it's as if there is a superimposed color or image on top of what is physically present. If, instead of looking outward, I'm staying inward or have my eyes closed, then I see images, words, or what you might think of as short films playing out, usually right at the center of my forehead. Since I understand what my imagination is capable of, I know that this is different. When in doubt, ask yourself if you could have made it up? Sure, it's always possible, and so is the possibility that you have a way of seeing the unseen.

Each person will have different levels of ability or skill with each of these ways of sensing the intangible world (you might have access to one or two of them, or all of them) and they can grow and develop over time with practice, and within safe, held space. Often our beliefs, or the lack of safety around claiming these ways of being in the world, get in the way of believing this can be true.

Dark Night Of The Soul

Oxford Languages defines a dark night of the soul as "a period of spiritual desolation suffered by a mystic in which all sense of consolation is removed." This period, while extremely challenging, is often a moment of death (a part of you, your psyche, or ego is dying) and spiritual birth or re-birth, where the person who is submerged and immersed in the darkness discovers new capacities, especially when they find people who know how to help them navigate this tender place of transition and emerge again. In this way, the person may or may not be a "mystic" as this rite of passage occurs to many (though perhaps we are all mystics) and yet the person usually returns as a healer of some sort as they now have deep wisdom to share and likely more capacity to help others navigate similar uncharted waters.

Divination

Divination is often defined as seeking or receiving knowledge about the future and/or the unknown through an intermediary object. Some people work with pendulums, shells, stones, dandelion seeds, runes, Tarot cards, mirrors, tea leaves, and many other tools designed for this purpose. From a healing perspective, divination is not about fortune telling, but a way to receive clues and insights into your own psychology, energy, path, or to receive information about practical medicine, actions, and ways to incorporate the clues you receive into your life and Self, should you choose to.

I know someone who does this to find which flower essences to give to a client. She holds a pendulum in one hand and knows which way it swings for "yes" and which way for "no" and then puts her other hand on each essence bottle. After she's touched each essence, a couple have always received a "yes" and they are what is needed. Divination is an augmented intuition, which some see as an interaction with spirit and others see as working with your own consciousness and energy or that of the person/people you are with. It's another way to work with "invisible" energies or vibrations and have them communicate in some way. This communication is then up to the interpretation of the person receiving it. Ultimately, the decision of what to do with the information (to feel if it resonates and take it or leave it) is up to the individual the divination is for. You can also do this for yourself.

Guides

Guides are spiritual helpers and have many names and forms. Some people and traditions call on spirit guides from each of the four cardinal directions (East, South, West, North) as well as the sky and all that is above, the earth and all that is below, and the ether or center in which all is possible. Others call upon benevolent ancestors, angels, archangels, ascended masters (meaning those who have either departed life or who have completed their work on earth and live in/as spirit), plant spirit guides, animal spirit guides, mineral or crystal guides, elemental beings or devas, and the list goes on. However a guide appears to you is exactly right and they are there to be called upon in ceremony and/or in your daily life. Some people work with their clair senses to feel, see, hear, and receive messages from these guides.

Plant Spirit

The concept of a plant spirit is difficult to put into words because it can be experienced in so many different ways. To me, plant spirits are the consciousness and essence of a plant—that which is not embodied in a physical form and yet is integral to their being. Think of your own spirit. What does the word 'spirit' mean for you? Maybe you think of spirit as the energy or quality which animates your body, a vibration in your heart, the part of you that connects to some larger energy or life force. Beyond the energy of the physical plant, the spirit has the ability to move and be moved, and to communicate in many ways that we can see, hear, feel, or sense in some way (and often ignore). Connecting with a plant is important because you can gain a sense of what spirit means for you, and how to work with plants individually and collectively.[3]

Reiki

The word Reiki and the technique most practitioners

work with comes from Japan. In Japanese, "rei" means spirit and "ki" means life force energy. Other words for "ki" that you may be familiar with are chi or prana. I like to imagine Reiki as a big ball of universal or life force energy. That's simplifying things because universal energy is everywhere but go with me on this visual. Imagine that there is a big ball of energy hovering above you or in front of you and generally you have access to some of it—your own life force energy, for example. Reiki practitioners can access a bit more of this big ball of energy. Imagine someone reaching up to the ball and creating a line or connection to it. Some way of bringing a part of that energy down, into the body and help it move or flow in themselves, another person, an animal, or plant. This is offered by laying hands either directly on the body or above, and can also be offered from a distance.[4]

Reiki Symbols

There are many different symbols with which Reiki practitioners work. Some are Japanese or Sanskrit characters; others are simple patterns that can be drawn or brought to mind easily. Each symbol has a specific purpose or way to amplify Reiki energy. For example, there is a symbol associated with distance Reiki, another to enhance working on an emotional level, one to give a boost of power, and too many others to name. As Reiki continues to evolve, more and more symbols appear and are added to the healing modality.

Shadow/Shadow Work

On an individual level, the shadow is an unconscious, repressed and/or unwanted aspect of yourself or your psychology. This also applies to the collective where repression is a part of the dominant way of being, or we turn away from that which makes us uncomfortable and what we don't want to see. The shadow on any level is what you sweep under the rug to not see it or have to deal with right away, but it's always there and, if not faced, will certainly deal with you. The unconscious or shadow wants to be acknowledged and will project and cast itself over and over again into life through repetitive behaviors, thoughts, interactions, and relationships, as it begs for acknowledgment, attention, and love. Shadow work is that of bringing what is unconscious into conscious awareness so that these aspects of self and society can be seen, honored, admitted entry, and even loved.

The Tarot

Whether the origins of the Tarot were from ancient Egypt, had Sufi roots, a blend of these, or from some other origin, all sources seem to agree that the information was codified and systematized in a deck of 78 cards in Italy in the early fifteenth century.[5],[6] These are broken up into two sets of cards: the Major Arcana and Minor Arcana and the deck as a whole was used as playing cards in a game which resembles bridge. The cards are also worked with for divination. As a result, the Tarot has a long and varied history with different beliefs and biases placed upon it. I am going to do the same —to describe the Tarot, and a Tarot reading, from a modern healing perspective through the next few definitions.

Tarot: Major Arcana

Arcana is the plural of the word arcanum and is derived from the Latin word *arcanus*, meaning "secret." The Merriam-Webster dictionary definition currently reads that arcanum is "mysterious or specialized knowledge, language, or information accessible or possessed only by the initiate" and that the word "entered English as the Dark Ages gave way to the Renaissance. It was often used in reference to the mysteries of the physical and spiritual worlds." This timing parallels that of the Tarot being systematized through the cards, so it makes sense that the word "arcana" came to describe the cards themselves as holding or containing this specialized knowledge.

The Major Arcana is a term associated with the Tarot cards that do not fall into a suit (otherwise known as the Minor Arcana) and are numbered zero through twenty-one. Each card represents and depicts a different archetypal energy. How you work with these archetypes is up to you, be it as a way of seeing a psychological belief or structure you hold or need more of, karmic lesson or influence, and/or viewing the Major Arcana as a journey through a cycle of evolution (if followed in numerical order you would move from The Fool as card zero through to The World as card twenty-one, representing completion or the all/everything only to potentially start all over again as The Fool).

In a reading, these cards can be pulled in any order and represent what you are working with in the present, what you are working towards, or what you may need to shift, transform, and release. All of us embody all of the archetypes represented in the Major Arcana and it becomes a matter of learning how they show up for you. Holly talks more about this and her role as a Tarot reader in our conversation.

Tarot: Minor Arcana

The Minor Arcana are 56 cards in a Tarot deck that are often seen as having to do with your daily life or the details of your psychology, spirit, and being. Minor doesn't mean "less than," nor does Major mean that they more important. The Minor Arcana cards are broken out into suits or themes. Here is an overview of each:

The Suit of Cups represent your feelings, emotions, creativity, and intuitive life. You can also associate them with the water element.

The Suit of Pentacles represent your work, relationship to money, and what you manifest or bring into the world. You can also associate them with the earth element.

The Suit of Swords represent your thoughts and actions and often have to do with ideas, decisions, and how you approach yourself and others through your thoughts. You can also associate them with the air element.

The Suit of Wands represent your internal energy sources, motivation, passion, and what you do with it that energy for yourself and in your life. You can also associate them with the fire element.

Tarot Reading

A Tarot Reading is the act of pulling from the deck one or more cards either for yourself, another person, group of people, situation, or otherwise, with a particular question or intention in mind. If there is no specific question or intention, then that becomes the intention: to see what comes. Based on the reader's intuition, understanding of psychology and energy, and ability to work with the clair senses, an interpretation of the card or cards occurs through a conversation. If you're reading for yourself, perhaps you think about the cards, tell a friend, journal, draw, sing, dance, or find your own way to interact with the messages. This is a mix of practical knowing, creative knowing, and intuition and is meant as a self-reflective tool for the person receiving the reading. Only they will know what resonates or feels accurate.

The Tarot reader is not there to be all-knowing and the more they can step out of themselves, and out of any egoic tendencies to predict, be right, or try to inflict their will, the more open and receptive both reader and recipient can be to the information laid out before them. All is open to interpretation and the act of even seeing the cards starts an internal psychological and energetic process to which you may be unaware.

HOLDING SPACE TO HEAL

N ow that you have the background, context, and key concepts, I'd like to welcome you into the conversation with Holly Ramey. As you read our exchange, notice any times when you feel inspired, called to act, agitated, angry, hopeful, or any other emotion that rises within you. I invite you to consider these emotions, thoughts, and any new ideas that emerge, so that you can continue the conversation in your own way once you've finished this book.

Seeking Connection

HEATHER SANDERSON: Welcome everyone. I'm here today with Holly Ramey. Holly has done so many interesting, marvelous, and fantastic things, which include studying yoga, meditation, Reiki, Tantra, Tarot, and plants—there are many healing arts that this wonderful soul has found her way into and with which she has created new offerings. We'll explore many of the ways that she's sharing her expertise and skills with the world.

Holly, since you have traversed so many worlds, I thought we could start with what I see as the midpoint, which feels like the Tarot part of your journey. Can you share a little bit about what drew you to the Tarot?

HOLLY RAMEY: That definitely would be around the midpoint. I had already been studying yoga for over five years, as well as my Reiki training. For those of you who don't know anything about Reiki, in level one you learn how to give Reiki to yourself and to other people and then in level two you're introduced to symbols. One of the symbols allows you to give distance Reiki—so Reiki to someone who is not in the same room as you. It also helps you travel through time and space, because energy is just energy and there are no limitations. This was something that felt insane to me, although really interesting and I was a little bit afraid of it.

I didn't know if I wanted to travel through time and space. Even after I was initiated into a level two Reiki training, I didn't use the symbols. I put them on a shelf and thought, "I don't know about these symbols. They seem cool, but I just don't know if they're for me." I didn't feel connected to them, but then the Tarot came, and it was all symbols, and they were symbols that I recognized.

I don't know why a part of me recognized them. It was as if I had been reading them all along and I just didn't know it. To meet the symbols on the Tarot cards was like being reintroduced to an old friend. Like when you re-meet someone and their life is totally different from when you knew them before. They look totally different. They're a whole new person, but there's some recognition there. That was what drew me to the cards.

When I had my first Tarot reading and saw the cards laid out in front of me, it resonated and I thought, "Oh yes, this is definitely something that I must do." Within a few months of receiving a reading, I signed up for a six-month intensive study and journey through the Tarot.

HS: It really called to you then. I love how quickly you went from "this is new information that feels like an old friend" to "I'm in it. Bam. Let's start."

What was that training like for you? How did the teacher approach it? Or how did you receive the information?

HR: I joined the Brooklyn Fools which was created by Jeff Hinshaw. He is an amazing Tarot teacher and astrologer, and he co-hosted it with Boccara Winter. They created a six-month container[7] where they held the space for us to explore each one of the Major Arcana cards. We met weekly and sat in the energy of each card through various forms, including meditation, sharing, altar building, sitting in circle, and community. There was traditional learning, like reading books and things like that, but it was very visceral. For example, we went to a church, and we spoke to a priest when we sat in the energy of The Hierophant. We went to a yoga shala, and we sat with the guru when we learned about The Hermit. It was very experiential.

HS: It sounds like it was a way of embodying what could

be just flat or non-dimensional and then seeing that these energies are in the world.

HR: And alive and within us because they are archetypes, and we all stand in all of these archetypes all of the time. Throughout our lives and various moments, we step into these "roles."

HS: Where did learning this take you next on your journey?

HR: Well, at first, I didn't envision myself being a professional Tarot reader. At that time, I was still in the yoga game. I was teaching ten classes a day: group classes and private lessons, all over New York City.

I'm not sure if this was around the time I was opening Medicine Space, which was a little healing center of my own, but I was starting to look beyond the yoga class, because there's only so much you can do in a yoga class. Though I still love the practice of yoga, I wanted something to connect a little bit deeper and explore the darker side of the psyche.

I felt that the opportunity for deeper intimacy was lacking in my practice and my classes. I was also starting to explore holding space for darkness, and what I loved about the cards is that they were not all love and light. They were The Devil and The Tower and these shadow energies that I think that yoga represents, as well. All of the healing practices that I've explored are, to me, more about embracing the shadow and the moon side of yourself.

That is what really drew me to work with the

Tarot and want to give readings and incorporate it into my workshops. I first started incorporating Tarot readings into my Reiki sessions because it was a way to look beyond the surface level of a session.

HS: It sounds like that was something you were also yearning for in your own healing path.

HR: Yeah, absolutely.

Holding Space For Darkness And Light

HR: After I found Reiki, I went down a deep well of my own. It came right after I finished my Saturn return which, for those who aren't into astrology, is around the time you're twenty-seven/twenty-eight years old. Saturn returns to where it was when you were born. Saturn is a fierce structural energy that tends to show us lessons that we need to learn.

So, I went through my Saturn return. It was horrendous. It was full of grief. I lost my brother to suicide right around when my Saturn return started and that was really a pivotal shift for me. When your heart breaks, it breaks open and we have to explore that wound. For me, there was a lot of darkness. There was a lot of heavy grief and then a lot of light shed on the patterns that had existed in my life and my family that were not normal. I think that when we have these patterns, and these unconscious behaviors, and we just live in this world, we think that it's normal because it's what we know.

When the veil lifts, you can see this is actually trauma. It is not normal. It creates a dark night of the soul.

HS: Thank you for sharing that so openly and so honestly. It's interesting to hear you speak about it now, at this point in your process, because it sounds like such a deep dive down into this dark well, as you said. What I'm hearing you also say, now that you've reached this point in your journey, is that there is so much light in how you're even sharing it with us right now. And it feels like a blending of the two—the light and dark—that have emerged from your deep, deep dive. Does that resonate?

HR: Fully. I'm so grateful that I was in this space, that I was in this wonderful community in New York, and that it was very magical and serendipitous. That even though I was in a time of deep darkness and healing, I was also in a space and healing community where I walked to get coffee in my neighborhood in Brooklyn, walked into a little shop, and saw a business card with symbols on it: a cup, a sword, a pentacle, and a wand.

I don't know why, but I picked it up and thought, "this is something I need to look into." And it's a business card of the Tarot reader. So, I think there's always light. It's just that we've got to pay attention to it. We've got to stay open to it. For me, finding the Tarot was the representation of that darkness, and the Tarot was a tool that reflected back to me what I was seeing and what I was feeling and made me feel hopeful. Our shadow is our shadow until we shed light on it, and then it's not.

HS: I like how you described the Tarot too, because it's not ignoring the darkness. It's saying that it's part of us. It's a part of life and let's jump into it. Let's experience it in some way and not pave over it, as some practices tend to, and that's often referred to as "spiritual bypass," or that idea of "let me just go around this darkness over here and pretend I'm always in the light." That feels like it could be a pattern that might not be helpful in the long term.

HR: It's not like we mean to do it, but we want to be popular, and we want our students to like us and to think our classes are fun and cool, so we can keep our numbers up and keep our job at the yoga studio. There can be this way that a yoga class becomes dogmatic, depending on what tradition you're studying. There is this sense of right and wrong. How is that any different than religion and all the other things that I rebelled against?

You also have an hour with a yoga class, and it becomes almost like choreographing a dance class. There's the music and the theme and the perfect transition from one posture to the next. We can lose a sense of intimacy or presence. Even though at its core, that's what the practice is meant to do: bring us into our own sense of presence and movement with our body, with our mind, and with our breath. But it can get lost. It can get lost in the mix of things. The

Tarot is raw and there is nowhere to go. It's just you and another person. You throw down the cards and that's it.

You can get lost in a little bit of performance art there, too, if you want to have the goal of your client being happy with the experience, but it's a lot harder to do.

HS: Because the cards are right there in front of you?

HR: Yes—you can only sugarcoat The Devil so much.

Reading The Tarot

HS: In working with the Tarot, have you ever experienced something that made you think, "Whoa, wait. What is happening right now?"

HR: Yeah, I mean almost every reading you have that moment where you think, "Oh God, what is this?"

What I love about it too is that there are 78 cards in the deck, and you can pull them upright or reversed. You can pull them in a million different combinations, so you may never read the same card in quite the same way for the same person. You're always being surprised. It's a dance. It's a dance of being able to stay open, stay curious, step out of your ego, stay present, and hold space for what the person in front of you needs.

But yes. Yes, is the answer to that question. I'm surprised sometimes and have to get out of what I know to allow for new information to come in. Because if I just stuck to what I read in the guidebooks, it would be pretty flat.

HS: It sounds intuitive.

HR: Totally.

HS: You've learned so much, but it also sounds like it's coming from you and your own sense.

HR: Definitely. And it also comes from the client and how engaged they want to be, how open they are to the experience, and how their guides may come through. It's a relationship in that moment.

HS: It sounds very energetic. I can see how Reiki could relate to it as an energy practice.

HR: Fully. When I'm offering Reiki, I'm already going into the energy field and working with the guides and the guardians. I'm a clairsentient, so everything is very strong in the way that I feel it through the body, rather than a clairvoyant. My teacher of Reiki was very much a seer, so she sees the aura colors, and that's the way she taught, but that's not the way I experienced it.

So the Tarot was also a way for me to tell my client, "This is what I'm feeling in my physical body," but with the Tarot then I could say, "What is this that I'm feeling in my body?" and pull some more Tarot cards to gain a deeper understanding and have more conversation to give them some practical tips and tools of how to work with the balancing of one of their chakras, for example.

HS: Also, bringing it into everyday life. All these things that can seem a bit "out there." I like that.

Creating Ceremony And Community

HS: You also offer ceremonies around the new moon, full moon, and the solstices and equinoxes. How did that start for you?

HR: I learned about ceremony from my Reiki teacher Deborah Hanekamp. Now her name is Momma Medicine. She had a physical space in New York where we met and I started doing ceremonies there with her.

They were these little ceremonies in a basement in Brooklyn that she would have once or twice a month and they were always really sweet. I enjoyed learning and doing healing work in community. The yoga teacher trainings are like that. Everything I've done is like that. It became interesting to learn about the phases of the moon and to see how, especially back then, I never wanted to get out of my bed on the full moon. There was all this intensity at that time.

Deborah would do a little bit of Reiki and healing work. She would do a bit of channeling messages for the energy of that particular moon. She didn't talk too much about the astrology, but just more about the phases of the moon, and it was always so nice and so sweet to sit in community with others.

I didn't start offering my own ceremonies until I moved to Nashville. I left my New York community behind and I had my daughter two weeks after we moved. She was a preemie, at two months early. At the time, I felt kind of uprooted: I had no family, no friends, no work community. So I think that I started offering these ceremonies because I was lonely and really wanted that sense of holding space and community again.

HS: That sounds like it's been of service for so many reasons. It's beautiful. I love that when you didn't have community around you, you decided to build it.

HR: It's hysterical because I didn't have a space, so I started them in a chiropractor's office in downtown Nashville. There was an alleyway behind it called Printers Alley. At 7:00 PM the country dive bars would open and there'd be honkytonk music and cigarette smoke coming up through the window. I moved them around to a bunch of different spaces and now they're just in the virtual space, but they've been such a bright light in 2020.

HS: As you described that, I really got a sense of walking between worlds. Like all of this other stuff happening in the physical world right outside your window, and yet you're here, connecting with the cosmos or lunar energies and holding space for other people in this deep, meaningful way. I love seeing both of those worlds very, very presently together because it feels true of every day.

HR: Totally! And it was scary too because Nashville is the South. I worried about how I was going to be received in this space after leaving New York City and starting to do these practices in a place where I'd be pulling into downtown and would see that there's a gun show and I'd think, "Oh shit, we're not in Kansas anymore." You have to go and be open and build it and they will come.

The Role Of Doubt And Authenticity

HS: Did you ever experience doubt?

HR: I still do. I'm still actively, always, doubting. All of it.

HS: And continuing to move forward. What drives that forward motion? Do you know?

HR: It hard because it's difficult to pick up and move somewhere and leave your community behind. I've definitely doubted that decision. Nashville was a hard move for me. It uprooted me and it made me really look deeply at myself. Moving to Nashville almost felt like a second Saturn return. It threw me into another dark place. Becoming a new mom is also a really hard thing, but then doing that when you left your community behind is another layer. So yes, I've doubted it deeply because it took me into another kind of dark night of the soul and I still do doubt. We still talk about moving back to New York, because that still feels like home to me.

There's nothing to do but lean in. The more you resist, the more it persists. But, to be honest, I fought all the changes pretty hard.

I feel like I really tried to recreate my New York life here and the universe is just like "No, you can't do that. You have to strip it down." So that's what I feel like I've been doing for four years. Really stripping everything down in a way and learning a bit more authenticity, a bit more of what my voice is versus what are the voices of other people. Where am I shapeshifting, and all new lessons that had to come in and be learned.

HS: I was struck by you sharing that word "authenticity" because, as we've been creating this together in this moment, what I'm hearing so strongly is this journey for authenticity and stepping more and more into yourself. That's what I see. Then offering that medicine to other people through blending so many of these skills that you've developed and worlds that you've been a part of, and now yes, finding your own way.

How is that now transforming your work?

HR: I recently shifted my work completely because of that. I felt really wrapped up in the idea of right and wrong and was thinking about the poem, "Out Beyond Ideas," by Rumi that says:

> Out beyond ideas of wrongdoing and rightdoing
> there is a field. I'll meet you there.
> When the soul lies down in that grass,
> the world feels too full to talk about.
> Ideas, language, even the phrase 'each other'
> doesn't make sense.

I felt like I was living in these ideas of wrongdoing and rightdoing and I was so afraid of doing the wrong thing. Saying the wrong thing. Not doing it perfectly. Not being perfect or right or good, and I had to strip away what all of that meant to me and why I even felt that what I was doing could be wrong. I don't know where I got that idea in the first place, and it started to not make sense. It took a lot of self-reflection to see that I was putting too much emphasis on the tool and not on the space.

What I wanted, more deeply than anything, was to connect, but all these things were in the way. All the things that we put in between us and another human being, so I rebranded all of my work. I don't want it to be about a Tarot reading or a Reiki session or a yoga class because I don't want it to be too focused on the expectation of those things.

What I really want it to be is a Spirit Session where we sit down together (and yes, I use all of those tools and maybe more), but the focus is on us connecting. Maybe we're connecting spirit-wise, maybe it's mind-body. It felt like there was too much noise and I wanted to get down to baseline and let it be more about two people together and holding space for each other.

I don't have to give you all the perfect tools because you are not a problem for me to fix. That came from me figuring out that my life isn't a problem to be fixed and I need to stop approaching it that way, because it left out compassion and a lot of humanness and messiness exists beyond right and wrong.

HS: I was so moved in my heart as you were speaking. My heart was right there with you because it sounds so healing to be offering in this way and holding that space for other people as you have been held, and maybe still want to be held. Beautiful, Holly.

HR: Thank you.

HS: How can people work with you in this way?

HR: You can go on my website: www.hollydramey.com.
I put up a whole page about Spirit Sessions, what they are and how we do it. Everything is virtual and the beauty of that is that I can work with anyone from anywhere in the world. Like we were saying, distance Reiki energy can travel through any time and space, so there are no limitations there.

It is again a way to have that community that I've been longing for, that I feel really my soul has been longing for my whole life. I think that I remember a time when we were all living in community. A time when things were less individualized and nuclear and there was more togetherness.

HS: I hear you, Holly, and hold that vision—and admire that you are finding ways to recreate that village albeit in very new ways to what your soul may remember from the past.

Plant Spirit Reading

HS: Part of these conversations is a plant spirit reading. The plant that has revealed itself to work with you in some way is a plant that I am not familiar with, other than knowing her name and what she looks like, but maybe you are. It's Angelica.

HR: In essential oil form, I've worked with her.

HS: Oh, interesting. That's great that you're already connecting in that way. I'm going to share a little bit about what I know about her, and maybe there are things that come up that you also know, or that will be revealing at this moment.

Even in the word "Angelica," there's an association with angels and working with guides or archangels or however you want to see that energy, but she holds an essence of light, with guidance and support and is known as a carrier of light. Which only just now, as I'm saying that, I'm thinking of the story you've shared and how being the one who brings light or finds the light in the darkness feels like a big part of your authentic offering in yourself and this journey you've been on. Maybe Angelica's always been there, or maybe she's coming through right now for some reason.

She also can help when you feel cut off from your inner Self, so a great ally for that internal support, or bolstering, that we sometimes need along the way. Maybe when there is doubt or that feeling of being lost. She's a huge inspiration, a beacon of light and supportive "go, go, go, you've got this" spirit and attitude.

HR: Plant cheerleader!

HS: Plant cheerleader, totally. For any of these ideas or inspirations that you want to bring into the world, she's there. She's got you.

HR: I love that. How did she come through? Did you do a little meditation?

HS: I did! Sometimes these plants come through or appear to me for people immediately. For example, when someone agrees to do the podcast, the plant's energy is right there in my mind or I sense it around me or see an image of it. That didn't happen this time. Even this morning, I was wondering if a plant would appear, and I felt a bit of that doubt you were talking about creep in. What if a plant doesn't appear? I cleared away that doubt by reaffirming that it would happen and, just before we started, I asked again for a plant that wanted to come and work with you, and then Angelica appeared and said, "it's me!"

I see things quite often and right at my third eye center. This was like a firework explosion of seeing the flower of Angelica right at that center … as though the image of her was superimposed upon any other thoughts or fluctuations of my "regular" mind. Since I'm not as familiar with her, I did a bit of research to see what she is all about and it felt right.

HR: That's so funny. I work with goddess cards and the goddess card that I pulled for this month for myself: Aeracura. She's a goddess I have never heard of, and her medicine is all about blossoming and it said to work with flowers, flower essences, flower essential oils, any kind of flower medicines, so I love that.

HS: That's so perfect. Maybe she can join you in some watery element as well.

HR: Yeah, oh always, always in the bath.

HS: Well, thank you so much, Holly. I appreciate your time and how openly you've shared so much of your story and your offering with us.

HR: Thank you for having me. I loved it.

CONCLUSION

When there is a lack of safety in the space around us, whether it stems from the family structure or household, unsupported early childhood experiences, or trauma at any life stage, we learn to cope in a myriad of ways. Often this means generating a false web of light around and through the entire body to feel safe and protected which can also show up as being "the good one," or "the brave one," or any other archetype you can imagine that embodies this false light. This lack of safety can also present itself in the other extreme: to abandon all light and hope, to swath yourself in an abundance of darkness, and feel that there is no light or you can interact with life as "the outcast," or "black sheep." Neither approach is sustainable in the long-term, nor is it true safety. Yet, we do this to survive difficult or harmful experiences. This is entirely natural and, in time, the corners of these ways of being start to erode.

Holly talked about this in relation to her ideals of perfectionism. When she was ready, she sought and found supportive structures of yoga, Reiki, Tarot, teachers and community which built up to generate a safe, held space (both externally and internally) so that she could then explore the shadow side of herself. Through this investigation, she saw that which she took on and held in herself because of her experiences. The more she worked with both the darkness and the light, and shed what was not hers to hold onto, the more she grew both her authentic Self and the safety she required within herself to move beyond the concepts of "right and wrongdoing," and the archetypes that were running her life. That which had a hold over her, in time, transformed so that it was either released or so that she became more than what she was holding onto. No longer governed by it. When these tendencies reappear, she has more information about what she requires to move through them: ceremony, community, and connection.

In building the safe container of this book to hold all that Holly shared, it's helped me explore more deeply what it means to be vulnerable, and the vital importance of holding space for one another. I've come away with a new understanding that when you are held, you can discover what it is that you are holding onto. You don't need to name it, but you might feel it, or a fraction of it. When you are held in a safe and supportive way, repeatedly and over time, you can then process whether a thought, emotion, belief, traumatic experience, pattern, or behavior has a hold over you. Does holding on hold you back in a way that is painful? Can it be released from your body and being into the larger container or the energetic field of space and time which we all share? Or, if you are exploring on your own, can you become a witness who allows things to be, while at the same time, learns to discern what serves you and what you no longer want to hold? Are you always holding onto the light or an ideal of who you need to be, and would having a safe space to explore your shadow help you let go of what it is you hold onto as exclusively true or "right"?

Since the container of holding space is neutral, any energy released into it is no longer fed and may even be met with unconditional love. Unconditional love is another powerful way to hold space for yourself and for others. Whether you are held with neutrality, compassion, radical acceptance, or fierce love, whatever you are holding will be transformed, as will you. As layers of holding release, you generate more space within yourself, uncover more parts of who you truly are, and even find that you can stay present. The safer you feel to be yourself, the more likely you will be to share that Self with the world, and to speak up or hold a space of safety for another: be it a person you've never met before and encounter on the street, or a friend or family member. Holding space has the power to be exponential and, once one person knows the way, it creates a chain reaction for others to experience and heal.

To that end, it's important to note that holding space isn't necessarily reciprocal—not everyone is able to offer it to themselves or another in every situation. It requires knowing yourself and your own capacity. Through this process you learn when you are able to be present with another person and you are unable to do so. To know that both are okay. When you do offer to hold space, it's important to do so without the expectation of anything coming back your way. Someone may require being held a thousand times before trusting that even a tiny part of themself is safe; for others it may take longer. Some may learn, through healing, what prevents them from feeling safe in their body, energy, Self, or life, and to translate this into holding space for others while some people may not. It's all okay and any sense of psychological and emotional safety that someone generates within their own body emanates subtly out into the world and can be felt by others. This makes me wonder what the world would be like if everyone felt safe all the time. What we could create and become with a world like that! The possibilities are endless.

Furthermore, what if holding space for one another generates that field of energy beyond right doing and wrongdoing of which Rumi speaks? What does it look like to exist there? I like to hope that it's where we can reconstruct the lost village that Holly longs for; a place where we can re-connect with ourselves and one another with respect, growth, and honoring both the shadow and the light equally. To re-imagine what community is as we move forward through space and time—what do we want it to be? It's up to us to build it.

OVER TO YOU

F eel inspired? Curious? Vulnerable? Want to explore what it means to hold space further? Try the exercises on the following pages to explore these concepts further. See what it is that comes to the surface for you in this moment. Your answers may change over time.

HOLDING SPACE
FOR YOURSELF

Think of a moment when you felt truly safe or supported. What did that feel like in your body? If you have no such moment to draw upon, that's okay. Imagine what you need right now. Draw or write the answers on this page.

ARCHETYPAL ENERGY

What is one archetype with which you identify? How does this energy play out in your life? What is the opposite energy or archetype? Once you have them, write, draw, sing or dance a conversation between the two. See what emerges.

SHADOW WORK

Think and feel into a time of darkness or the ways you avoid the shadow parts of yourself. What are they? Draw or write about those parts of yourself. Then, draw or write the ways in which they can be loved.

CLAIR SENSES

What clair senses do you have access to? Which are you afraid of? Do you believe that they are real or not? Are there some you wish you had? Write about them, then explore your relationship to these ways of being in the world.

CEREMONY

Write down one intention that you would like to explore further. Create a safe space, invite any guides or helpers to assist you, then speak your intention out loud. See what comes.

My intention is to _____.

AT A DISTANCE

You can also hold space at a distance (by having the intention to do so) for a person, situation, land, or place in the world. Think of someone or somewhere you would like to hold space for. Write them down. Then, bring that person or place to mind. Notice what happens. Repeat as often as you'd like.

COMMITMENT

Make one commitment to yourself for how you will generate safety in the world. Write it down.

ACKNOWLEDGMENTS

A huge thank you to Holly Ramey for sharing her experience and wisdom now and always. I am constantly grateful that we sat together for breakfast that first day of retreat so many years (and what feel like lifetimes) ago, as we have traversed uncharted waters together time and time again.

I'd also like to thank Deanna McFadden for her constant encouragement and for our daily exchange of voluminous text messages, ideas, and unwavering dedication to one another's work, Vanja Adzovic for her keen editorial feedback and guidance. I love how Rasa Morrison was able to take a messy sketch of a unicorn and an owl, representing majestic wisdom, scribbled on the back of a notebook and turn it into the beautiful logo and cover image you see here.

Training with Dr. Clarissa Pinkola Estés has deeply influenced my writing and reinforced much of my understanding of healing psychology and energy through the physical experience of the body. Catherine Calderon first introduced me to the concept of archetypes and dancing with them (literally), and I feel the power of doing that dance in front of a group of women again now. And a big thank you to Carole Guyett for the three years of training in Sacred Plant Medicine, the encouragement to claim my medicine, and bring it into the world. Writing is a big part of that medicine and I am privileged to be able to focus time and energy into developing it. And, of course, with deepest respect, I honor the plants who truly are guiding it all.

ENDNOTES

[1] *Oxford Languages*

[2] *Merriam-Webster Dictionary*

[3] This excerpt can be found in each of Heather's Plant and Tree Spirit Short Reads. For more, visit, www.majesticwisdompublishing.com/books

[4] From *Building the Future Now Through Reiki: A Conversation with Nathalile Biermanns*

[5] Tarot: History, Symbolism, and Divination by Robert M. Place

[6] Mystical Origins of the Tarot: From Ancient Roots to Modern Usage

[7] A container in this sense means the entire time between the first and last class. This term is often used in conjunction with "holding space." The container is either the time, space, or both and the energetic and physical work done by those creating it to create a closed or contained environment in which participants feel safe to explore and learn. Even in a weekly class, each instance of class is held on its own and within the larger container of the entire course or semester.

ABOUT HOLLY

Holly Ramey is a writer, mom, yoga teacher, tarot reader/energy worker, and space holder who believes in magic. She loves to cook, garden, work with herbs, cast spells, write poetry, watch crazy documentaries, and explore the human psyche. You can find out more about her on her website, www.hollydramey.com, and follow her work on her Substack at Long Strange Trip.

ABOUT HEATHER

Heather Sanderson has written 20+ plant and tree spirit short reads, a collection of poetry, short healing arts books, several podcast episodes, hundreds of yoga classes and workshops, Reiki trainings, and plant spirit offerings. Trained in many healing arts disciplines, she focuses on bringing her magic and medicine to the world and encourages others to do the same. You can find her books at www.majesticwisdompublishing.com, her other work at www.journeythroughyoga.com, and follow her on Instagram at @heather.sanderson.

ABOUT MAJESTIC WISDOM PODCAST

Majestic Wisdom podcast invites you to remember your magic and bring it into the world, whatever it may be. Learn from the wisdom of others, and all the different ways there are to live a life, to engage with the world, and to create. Each episode also features a plant spirit teaching inspired by the guest. To listen to an episode, visit www.majesticwisdompublishing.com/podcast.

———

BOOKS BY THIS AUTHOR

Plant Spirit Short Reads
Dreaming with Dandelion
Dreaming with Elder
Dreaming with Heather
Dreaming with Holly
Dreaming with Goldenrod
Dreaming with Mugwort
Dreaming with Nettle
Dreaming with Red Clover
Dreaming with Rosemary
Dreaming with Sumac
Dreaming with Sunflower
Dreaming with Trillium
Dreaming with Violet

Tree Spirit Short Reads
Dreaming with Apple
Dreaming with Birch
Dreaming with Hawthorn
Dreaming with Oak
Dreaming with Redwood
Dreaming with Spruce
Dreaming with Willow

Healing Arts Short Reads
Loving Kindness for Everyday Life
Understanding Reiki
Yoga Nidra for Everyday Life

Poetry
Sister, (a collection of poems)

The Future is Possible Series
Building the Future Now Through Reiki: A Conversation with Nathalie Biermanns
Creative Being: A Conversation with Gérome Barry
Envisioning New Ecosystems: A Conversation with Stewart Hoyt
Holding Space to Heal: A Conversation with Holly Ramey
Nature Sanctuary for the Future: A Conversation with Marina Levitina

Visit www.majesticwisdompublishing.com to learn more.

Made in the USA
Middletown, DE
22 November 2022

15772200R00046